MW01519683

Written by Barrie Wade and Maggie Moore
Illustrated by Bethan Matthews

Collins Educational
An imprint of HarperCollinsPublishers

Mrs Smart

I'm used to someone being
sick in the coach on the
way to camp. I'm used to
coping with bumps and bites and
scratches. But I never expected a bad
accident! Mr Baker and I bring my class
here every year and nothing like this has
ever happened before.

Of course we have had a few problems
in the past and I thought this time we
might have a bit of trouble with Rachel.
She's not been having an easy time this
year. She's a lovely girl, really, but she
seems to find it hard to get on with other
people. I don't know what it is. Somehow
she stirs things up without meaning to,
and then gets upset herself afterwards. I
decided to put her in with Kim, Anna and
Sally. They're so easy to get along with,
and they're fun to be with, too. I'm

pleased that they *did* get on really well together. Rachel just can't help herself when she causes a bit of upset.

I hope it won't make any difference to the way people think about the school camp. It's the first time that some of the girls and boys have ever stayed away from home, so there's bound to be some strain. But it's so good for my class to come to the seaside in their last term before going to secondary school. There's so much to do and to learn!

There was the usual excitement and worry about sharing rooms and sleeping in bunks, but that's normal. We usually all have a good time. I enjoy it as much as anyone. Even doing jobs like the washing up can be fun. It was this time, too.

I'm glad it was nearly time to go home when the trouble came. This is the first time anything really serious has happened, and I don't suppose anyone could have seen it coming.

Kim

I was really disappointed at first because there were no tents. When they said it was a school camp, I thought we would sleep in tents and sit around campfires at night. "You can't camp without tents," I said.

"Yes, you can," said Mrs Smart, "and you'll like it."

I do like our room. I'm sharing with Anna, Sally and Rachel. I would rather have had a top bunk, but I'm in the bottom bunk across from Rachel. She grunts in her sleep and sometimes keeps me awake. The first night we didn't even try to sleep, though. Mrs Smart came in twice because we were giggling. The second time she was really cross. We were quieter after that, until I said, "What is small and green and goes camping?"

Sally said, "No idea."

"I don't know either," said Rachel.

"We give up," Anna said. "What is small and green and goes camping?"

"A boy sprout," I told them. They giggled and it set us all off again.

"A boy sprout! A boy sprout!" chanted Rachel. She jumped about, until our bunks rocked.

Soon Mrs Smart came in again. We heard her coming. I had my head under the covers, but she knew we were awake.

"Right," she said. "You four will do the washing up after breakfast tomorrow. Now get off to sleep. You're disturbing everyone."

It was hard not to giggle when Rachel kept whispering, "Boy sprout, boy sprout." We tried to giggle quietly under the covers.

The next day was great. It wasn't very sunny but it was warm. Mr Baker gave us a talk about keeping in a group and making sure we didn't get cut off by the tide. We all paddled in the water close to shore before we started collecting things. The sea was calm but cold. We found lots of pebbles on the beach. It was like hunting for treasure. Mrs Smart showed us how to look up the stones in a book. I found out the pink ones are called pink granite. They're washed right down the coast from the North-East of Scotland. My favourites, though, are the flints. They're dark grey and shiny with bits of white round them. The white bits are chalk. Flints are washed down from the sea bed off the Yorkshire coast.

We found lots of rocks called *gneiss*. Mr Baker spelled it for us. It looks hard, but you say it like *nice*. Mrs Smart told us it was formed by tremendous heat and pressure in the earth. We all put our stones and pebbles on the tables and made labels for them. I drew pink flowers on my label for the pink stones.

"That's nice," Mr Baker said.

"No, it's not, Sir," I said. "It's pink granite."

It's a shame that Rachel spoiled things right at the end of the day. I think she's really sorry for what she did, but she finds it hard to say so. Anyway, nobody expected him to act like that.

Rachel

He was sick near me on the bus and I hate that. It was his fault. He shouldn't have eaten all those crisps and, anyway, I didn't know about his mum then. Nobody tells me anything.

I wouldn't have said what I did if I had known. I'm sorry I pinched his stone. How was I to know it was the one he wanted to give to his mum? I only did it for a joke. I didn't know he'd go mad. He knocked all my pebbles on the floor and I had to sort them out again. It's a good job Mrs Smart helped me.

Then after dinner Mr Baker and Mrs Smart did the washing up and David and Ben did the drying. They were laughing and singing. Mr Baker wore his apron and he kept splashing Mrs Smart with water from the sink. I just said, "I think he really likes Mrs Smart." I didn't mean anything and, anyway, I was only talking to Sally. He just got up from the dinner table and ran out. That's when he locked himself in the toilet.

All Sally said at the time was, "Don't be daft. She's a lot older than him. Anyway, she's married." I wish someone had told me. Then I wouldn't have said what I did the next day.

We spent the morning looking at the plants that grow in different places. Some grow in fresh water and some grow on the saltmarsh. Some even grow on the sand dunes. Then, in the afternoon, when the tide was very low, we spent some more time looking for pebbles to add to our collections.

David had just found a pure white stone. It was oval shaped. He took it to Mr Baker.

"What's this one, Sir?" he asked.

"Beats me," said Mr Baker. "It's very light. I don't think it's stone. What do you think this one is, Mrs Smart?" he called to her. She went over to Mr Baker and that left us two together. I heard her say, "You're right. It's not a stone. This is what is left of a cuttlefish. It's just a skeleton, but budgerigars like it."

I could see they were just talking about the cuttlefish, but I said, "She really likes Mr Baker, too!"

I only said it to find out what he'd do.
I never expected him to run off again.
I wish somebody had told me about
his mum.

David

When he ran off, I went
after him. The others didn't
follow. He ran towards the
sea. I ran after him. I still can't run all that
fast, but then he stopped and I caught up
with him. He was throwing stones into the
waves and making them skim. I did the
same. We kept our eyes on the stones.
Most of them just plopped into the water.
He didn't say anything much. I just said,
"Good shot", when he made a stone
bounce. He did the same. "Good shot," he
said. Then suddenly he yelled, "Oh, no!
The tide!"

I had forgotten all about it, even though they had warned us the first day. I reckon the sea watches you, then creeps up behind you. We ran as hard as we could. He let me keep up, I reckon, but the sea had come behind us like a river. Later, Mr Baker told me it was called a *creek*. I was scared stiff. We were cut off, and the tide in the creek was flowing really fast. The

water looked deep. Mr Baker was on the other side, but he seemed a long way away. "I can't swim, Sir," I shouted.

For a moment we just stood and looked at each other. I can still remember how hard my heart was beating! Then, like a video starting after a pause, we were off running again.

"Run that way," shouted Mr Baker, pointing. We ran along the sand between the sea and the creek. Mr Baker ran along the sand on the other side and kept pace with us. The creek got narrower.

"I'm coming," Mr Baker yelled. Then he ran into the water. He's tall, but the water came right over his knees. He grabbed both of us, picked us up, and waded back through the water again. Do you know, he never even told us off.

Ben

I've never had a rabbit of my own. I used to look after the one in infant school, but Mum never let me have one. She said it was cruel to keep animals locked up. There are hundreds here. Most are brown, but a few are black. I was the first to see one.

"Look," I said, "a rabbit."

Mrs Smart is not really keen on them. "Yes," she said, "sand dunes are good places for rabbits to feed and make their burrows, but they cause a lot of damage by scratching and burrowing. They dig out plants from the sandy soil and that leads to erosion. Do you know what that is?"

I didn't, but I said, "Yes, Miss."

"Well," she went on, "the wind can then

blow away the sand and sometimes it makes large holes."

I reckon rabbits would have a tough time with Mrs Smart. She seems to care more about sand than about rabbits.

I reckon the rabbits have a tough time anyway. On our next-to-last day I was walking with Pete and suddenly this fox appeared on top of a sand dune. We stopped. It stopped, too, and looked straight at us. Then it backed away and disappeared. Seconds later it ran across the path ahead of us. I never knew foxes had white tips to their tails. This one did.

"See that?" said Pete.

"Yes," I replied, "it's after the rabbits."

I still like rabbits, even if their holes did cause Mr Baker to fall. You can't say it was their fault. They're only doing what rabbits do.

Sally

When I heard we were camping at the seaside, I wanted to go on the fairground. "I love roller coasters," I told Mrs Smart.

"But there's nothing like that," Mrs Smart answered. "It's just a sandy beach where we can collect pebbles and things. It'll be fun."

It was no fun at first, I can tell you. Pebbles are really boring, but then we found other things. I've got these lovely razor-shells and whelk shells that look like little helter-skelters. But the best bit was when Rachel and I found a dead crab. It was huge.

"We'll look it up in the book when we get back," Rachel said.

"No," I said, putting it carefully in my bag. "I've got a better idea."

It was me who put it in Mrs Smart's bed, halfway down where her feet would touch it first.

We kept listening for her to scream after bedtime that night. Her room is only down the hallway from where we are, so we should have been able to hear her, but nothing happened. We didn't hear a thing. We had a good laugh about it though.

Next morning at breakfast, she didn't seem to be cross. She talked about bird ringing and said that we would see how it was done later that day. Then she smiled and said, "Oh, and I want to thank the person who left me a present last night. It was a really kind thought."

So I reckon the crab did get her. She got me later, though, and I suppose that's fair.

Kulbir

It's been really hard for him.
I knew he was going to have
a new dad before he told
me. His mum told my mum and that's how
I knew. I'm his best mate, but he only told
me this week. It was after he was sick on
the coach. We stopped and Mr Baker took
him outside and walked up and down
with him until he felt better. He told me
afterwards when we were alone.

On our last day, we went to watch the bird ringing. We had to get up really early. He took his stone with him. It's a jasper and it's smooth grey sandstone with plum coloured veins running through it. He's going to give it to his mum. The bird ringers have fine nets they call mist nets. The birds can't see the nets, so they fly into them and get tangled up. It sounds cruel, but the birds are not hurt at all. They wouldn't let us hold the birds, though. You have to be trained to hold them properly, so you don't hurt them when you take them out of the net. We only saw one bird. The bird ringer said it was a chiffchaff. It was really tiny with dark legs that were thinner than matchsticks. The bird ringer measured it, weighed it, then fixed a tiny ring on its leg.

He was the one who kept asking questions. "Why do you do that?" he asked.

"Well," said the bird ringer, "every ring has a number so we can trace the birds later."

"Doesn't it hurt them?" he asked.

"No it doesn't. These are special rings made of aluminium. They're light and flexible, and fixed properly so they don't hurt. They won't even catch on twigs."

"Why do you call them *chiffchaffs*?" he asked. "It's a funny name."

"I suppose it is," said the bird ringer. "A lot of birds are named after the calls they make. Next spring or early summer, listen out for a bird calling *chiff – chaff, chiff – chaff* from the top of a tree. You can be sure it will be a chiffchaff that's come to spend the summer here."

"How far do chiffchaffs fly?" he asked.

"Well," said the bird ringer. "Chiffchaffs fly here from Africa to spend the summer, then they fly back."

"Wow," I said, "that's a long way."

"Yes, and the rings tell us how long birds live," the bird ringer said. "Not so long ago, a dead bird that was found in Africa had been ringed here ten years ago."

"Now we'll let this chiffchaff go. She needs to find her mate."

The bird ringer let us both stroke the chiffchaff gently with one finger tip. She just looked up at us. When we went outside, she stood on the bird ringer's hand for a bit, then flew off fast. We watched until she disappeared.

As we walked back, he was whistling.
I said, "So how do you feel about having
a new dad."

"Great," he said. "I'm really happy."

I was glad, because up to then I hadn't
been too sure.

Anna

I've found out so many things this week. For a start I never knew there were so many interesting pebbles. Then we saw a short-eared owl flying over the salt marsh. I never knew owls came out in the daytime. This one does. We watched it flying up and down over the marsh hunting for something to eat. Suddenly, it would swoop and disappear. I reckon it had a good feed that afternoon. Mrs Smart said owls like to eat the little voles that live on the marshes. Poor voles!

Then I learned to recognise different grasses and flowers. Some will only grow on freshwater marsh. Some will only grow where it's salty. But the butterflies and moths are my favourite. Sally and Rachel are scared of moths. I'm not. The best one is the cinnabar moth. It looks more like a butterfly, but it's a moth. It's a beautiful crimson and grey. It's really clever, too. It lays its eggs only on the ragwort plant because its caterpillars like to eat ragwort leaves. The caterpillars are stripy and brightly coloured so that the birds will think they taste nasty. I've found out a lot.

I've found out about people, too. I really get on all right with Rachel, though I didn't think I would. Mrs Smart has been good fun, too. She's a bit of a dragon in school and tells us off, but she was great about the crab. She wasn't cross. In fact, I think she liked the joke. But we never expected her to do what she did.

On the last night the four of us were really tired. Mrs Smart and Mr Baker gave us all a party and they did all the washing up and drying, while we played board games and cards. We wanted to help, but they wouldn't let us.

"Certainly not," Mr Baker said with a laugh as he put on a funny little apron. "Leave it to the experts." Then Mr Baker played his guitar and we sang all the songs we knew.

By the time we went off to bed, we were all feeling very sleepy. Back in our room, I

was ready to put the light out when
Rachel said, "I can't get into bed."

"I can't either," said Sally, "and I can't
find my pyjamas."

Then Kim and I found we couldn't get
into bed either.

"Somebody has turned our beds round,"
Rachel said.

"They've turned the mattresses round so
the pillows are at the bottom," said Kim.
"We'll have to sleep the other way round."

"But where are my pyjamas?" moaned Sally.

Then she found them inside her bed, but she couldn't get into them. Somebody had sewn up the sleeves and the legs. We began to giggle.

"Which of you did this?" cried Sally.

We all said it wasn't any of us and she believed us because she saw that the stitches were too neat. None of us could sew like that. It took us ages to unpick the tight little stitches.

Sally saw the joke and laughed with us.

"Well, she's got you back," said Kim.

"Yes, she's all right really," Sally said.

We giggled for a long time, but Mrs Smart never came in.

Mr Baker

I was looking forward to the week at camp. I thought I'd get a chance to talk to him more. I mean, I know how hard change can be, though so far we've got on really well. But things started to go wrong this week. It's not like him to run off or behave as he did. I think he must have got teased a bit. I know Rachel said something he didn't like, but he wouldn't tell me what.

I always try to be fair, so I don't want to treat him any differently from the others. I just kept in the background to be there if he needed me. He seems to understand that. He's usually very quick to understand how people feel. So I was surprised when he ran off the first time and locked himself in the toilet. I was hoping everything was sorted out, but then he ran down to the sea just as the tide was coming in. That could have been nasty! I began to wonder if I had said or done something to upset him.

When we'd got everyone to bed on the last night I went off for a walk. I went to think things over by myself. I walked down the track to the sea. It was calm and peaceful with the sea sounding like a lullaby. I climbed up a sand dune and looked over the beach. I could just see the line of white where the waves were breaking. I thought of him and Mary for a long time. I'm really looking forward to being part of a family.

It happened when I set off back to the camp. I ran down the side of the dune and suddenly felt a terrific pain. I had caught my foot in a rabbit hole that I hadn't seen in the dark. I've never broken a bone before, but I knew my leg had gone. I even heard the bone crack. I also knew I'd never make it back by crawling. It was too far.

I lay for a long time until I remembered my torch. I knew everybody was in bed, but I hoped somebody might see my signal. It's funny it happened to be Pete.

Pete

I think Gerry is great. Mum calls him that and I do, too. Only in school it has to be Mr Baker. I liked him when he was my teacher, but it's going to be strange when he gets married to my mum. It's a bit funny when I think about him as my dad. I didn't know what the others would say about it when they found out. I thought I'd be in my new school then, because they're not going to get married until the summer holidays. I was going to keep well away from Gerry this week. Then I was sick on the bus and he looked after me. He was really kind as usual. Everybody was looking at us through the window and I felt sure they all knew that he was going to be my dad. That made me feel funny, I don't know why.

I hadn't told Kulbir, but Rachel must have known somehow. She was really horrible. She pinched my jasper pebble and said horrible things. I went mad and ran off to stop myself from hitting her. Then the next day she said something horrible again. I could see she knew and she was doing it on purpose. So I ran off again. This time David came after me.

Gerry helped me again when David and I were caught by the tide. The trouble is, he's always helping me. That's why it was so good when I could help him for a change.

I don't know what made me look out of the window. I can see out from my top bunk just by moving the curtain. I saw the light straightaway.

"Hey, somebody's flashing a light," I said.

"Where?" Kulbir asked.

"Down on the sand dunes," I said.

The others came to look.

"It's a glow-worm," Ben said.

"Don't be daft," I said. "Glow-worms don't switch on and off."

"That's right," said David. "Somebody is signalling."

"Wait," I said suddenly. "Somebody is in trouble."

"How do you know?" asked Ben.

"Because they are. They're signalling in Morse code. Look. Three short, now three long, now three more short."

"What's that?" asked Ben.

"S.O.S.," I said. "It stands for Save Our Souls. Somebody's in trouble. Look, it's starting again."

"Quick," said David. "Let's get Mr Baker."

Gerry wasn't in his room, so we had to knock on Mrs Smart's door.

We told her about the flashing light and we all looked out at it.

"You're right, Pete," she said. "It is a signal. Get Mr Baker."

"He's not in his room, Mrs Smart," said Kulbir.

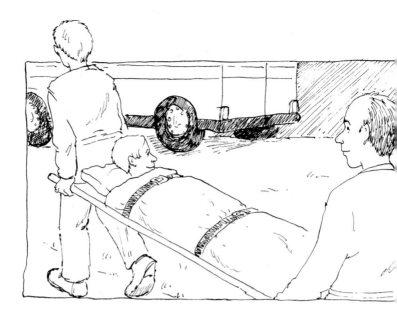

Mrs Smart suddenly looked worried. She woke the warden who got a big torch and set off down to the beach. He soon found Gerry and ran back. Then the ambulance came and they fetched Gerry up the path on a stretcher.

We went outside.

Gerry waved to us from the stretcher. His leg was broken. He was very brave, acting as if nothing had happened, but it must have hurt a lot.

"It was Pete who understood your signal," said Mrs Smart. "He knows Morse code."

"Yes, I taught him," said Gerry.

I said, "Can I come with you?"

"Sure," he said. "I'd like that."

So I got into the ambulance with him. I felt great that I'd managed to help him for once.

In the ambulance we had a really good talk.

Gerry started by saying, "Well, it looks like I'll have a plaster cast on my leg when your mum and I get married."

"Can I be the first to write my name on it?" I asked.

"Sure," he said.

In the hospital I wrote on the plaster, "To Dad. Get well soon. Love, Pete."

I don't care who sees it.